Great Scientific
Questions and the
Scientists Who
Answered Them

HOW DO WE KNOW

HOW STARS
SHINE

ALLAN B. COBB

Great Scientific Questions and the Scientists Who Answered Them

HOW DO WE KNOW
HOW STARS SHINE

THE ROSEN PUBLISHING GROUP, INC.
NEW YORK

Published in 2001 by The Rosen Publishing Group, Inc.
29 East 21st Street, New York, NY 10010

First Edition

Library of Congress Cataloging-in-Publication Data

Cobb, Allan B.
How do we know how stars shine / by Allan B. Cobb. —1st ed.
p. cm. — (Great scientific questions and the scientists who answered them)
Includes bibliographical references and index.
ISBN 0-8239-3380-6 (library binding)
1. Stars—Juvenile literature. [1. Stars. 2. Astronomy.] I. Title. II. Series.
QB801.7 .C63 2001
523.8—dc21

2001002004

Cover images: Interstellar clouds within the Lagoon Nebula, as photographed by the Hubble telescope.

Cover inset: radio telescope.

Manufactured in the United States of America

Contents

First Steps

Astronomy is the oldest of all the sciences and dates back thousands of years. Ancient peoples noticed that the stars in the night sky changed throughout the year. The patterns of stars in the sky followed a cycle. By making observations of where stars were in the sky, the first calendar was

created. The ancient Egyptians were probably the first to use the stars to make a calendar. The Nile River floods at a certain time every year. These annual floods deposited new layers of nutrient rich soil essential to farmers. As soon as the floods receded, the farmers planted their crops. It was important to know when the floods would come every year, and the stars in the night sky told the Egyptians the seasons. By 2780 BC, the Egyptians were able to calculate the length of a year to 365 days. This gave them a calendar and the ability to predict when the Nile floods would come each year.

The Greeks had a strong interest in science as a way of explaining nature. Astronomy was one of the sciences that attracted their interest. Their observations had a profound impact on how the stars were viewed.

Our ancient ancestors tracked the stars throughout the year and discovered that they followed a cycle. They used this knowledge to make the first calendars.

Greek astronomer and philosopher A n a x a g o r a s (500–428 BC) contributed much to early astronomy. He correctly explained the cause of lunar and solar eclipses. He also was the first to say that the Moon reflected sunlight rather than producing its own glow.

Plato's view that Earth was at the center of the universe persisted for 2,000 years.

The Greek philosopher Plato (428–348 BC) believed in the perfection of the heavens. In his view, Earth was at the center of the cosmos. All heavenly bodies were fixed to circular "spheres" that revolved around Earth. The universe was like an onion with Earth at the center and all heavenly bodies affixed to

Ptolemy furthered the concept that everything in the skies was attached to spheres that orbited Earth, which was thought to be at the center of the universe.

the outer layers. Plato's views were popularized by Aristotle (384–322 BC), and this concept of the universe dominated astronomical thinking for the next 2,000 years. The theory was given mathematical support by the Greek astronomer Claudius Ptolemy (AD 100–170).

Around 800 AD, the Arabs began making advances in astronomy. They devised instruments to

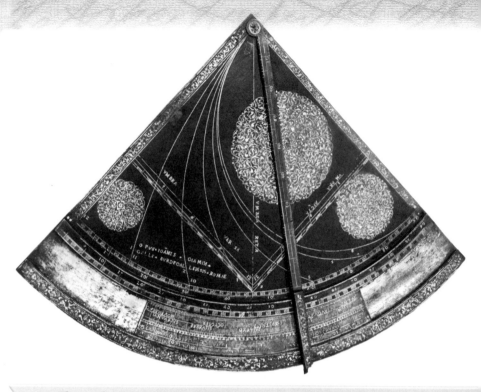

The Arabs invented instruments to locate and map the positions of stars. They also used sextants to measure the height of a star above the horizon. If the height was known at a specific time, the observer could determine his or her latitude.

help them accurately locate the position of stars and began to make the first maps of the night sky. The influence their maps had on astronomy lives on even today. They were the first to name many of the stars and the Arabic names are still used by astronomers. Their maps were accurate enough to be used for navigation. With their precise observations and mathematical skills, they refined some of the theories of the Greeks and rekindled interest in theoretical astronomy. A device called a sextant could be used to measure the height of a star above the horizon. If the height of a particular star above the horizon was known at a specific time, the observer could determine his latitude. Arab scientists such as Alhazen (965–1039) studied the magnifying effects of lenses and how light was reflected or refracted. Much early Greek science was preserved by the Arabs and found its way back to Europe at the end of the Dark Ages.

INVENTION OF THE TELESCOPE

In 1608, Dutch eyeglass maker Hans Lippershey (1570–1619) applied for a patent for a new optical device called a telescope. His telescope used two lenses in a tube to magnify distant objects. He is also credited with inventing the microscope, because if his telescope was reversed, it would magnify small

Galileo built a telescope in 1609 and made many contributions to astronomy. He studied mountains on the Moon, tracked stars in the Milky Way, and discovered four moons orbiting Jupiter.

objects that were very close. A telescope that magnifies an image through a series of lenses in a tube is called a refracting telescope.

Galileo Galilei (1564–1642) heard about Lippershey's telescope and built his own in 1609. He improved on the design and began making observations. This was not Galileo's first contribution to the science of astronomy. In 1604, he noted a new star that appeared in the constellation Ophiuchus. Galileo had witnessed a nova, or a stellar explosion. His calculations showed that the new star was much more distant than the planets, and that the current conception of the size of the universe ought to be enlarged. His results also showed that changes did indeed take place in the celestial regions. The cosmos was not, as the Greeks believed, perfect and unchanging. Armed with a telescope, Galileo began making more contributions to astronomy. He described the mountains on the Moon, the multitude of stars in the Milky Way, and the existence of four moons around Jupiter. He also noted the phases of the planet Venus, sunspots, the rotation of the Sun, and Saturn's rings. All of these accomplishments were made possible by his telescope. Galileo's telescope was not very powerful by today's standards. It was only about as powerful as a typical pair of binoculars.

Galileo also embraced the new heliocentric view of the solar system worked out by Nicolaus Copernicus

(1473–1543). Copernicus had noted that the orbits of Earth and the known planets could be more simply explained by a theory that the Sun was at the center of the solar system. This idea slowly replaced the concept that Earth was at the center of the universe.

In 1666, Isaac Newton (1642–1727), most famous for his

Copernicus studied the orbits of Earth and the planets, and theorized that the Sun was at the center of the solar system. This idea slowly replaced earlier beliefs that Earth was at the center of the universe.

17

discovery of the universal law of gravitation, became interested in optics and some of the problems observers were having with telescopes. When stars were observed with a telescope, they often had rainbow halos around them that obscured their images. Newton wanted to make a telescope that did not distort light in this way. To understand what was happening, he began to look at how light passed through a prism. Passing sunlight through a prism resulted in a rainbow of colors from red to violet. Newton determined that this happened because light was actually made up of different colors that were refracted, or bent, at different angles as they passed through the glass. This problem in telescopes is known as chromatic aberration. He found that there was no easy

To solve the problem of chromatic aberration, Newton designed a new type of telescope, called a reflecting telescope. Its design enabled astronomers to use observing instruments with high magnifications.

way to prevent this rainbow effect with the multiple lenses of a refracting telescope. His solution to the problem was to invent a new telescope that used a mirror to replace the primary lens. This new type of telescope was called a reflecting telescope. The design of the reflecting telescope allowed astronomers to build observing instruments that had very high magnifications but were still light enough in weight to be used effectively. The use of a prism to break down sunlight into its separate colors would eventually, as we shall see, provide the means to determine what the stars were made of.

Analyzing Light

2

The only way to examine a star is to study its light. Even the nearest star is so far away that it would be invisible to us if it were not for its brightness. In studying the stars, starlight is all we have to work with. Light is a type of energy in the form of electromagnetic waves. Other forms of electromagnetic

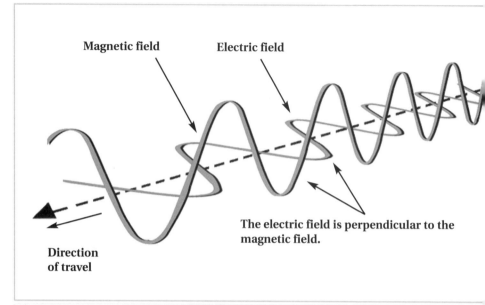

Magnetic field

Electric field

The electric field is perpendicular to the magnetic field.

Direction of travel

A light wave, or any other electromagnetic wave, consists of electric and magnetic fields vibrating at right angles to each other.

energy include radio waves, infrared and ultraviolet rays, X rays, and gamma rays. Electromagnetic waves do not require a medium to convey them, in the way that air molecules carry sound waves. Just how they propagate is still a mystery, but they can move through the vacuum of space at tremendous speeds—300,000 kilometers, or 186,000 miles, per second. Light waves are unique in that our eyes have evolved to detect them.

Light waves are created whenever electrically charged particles vibrate. Since the atoms of all substances are surrounded by shells of negatively charged electrons, all substances are capable of giving off light. The color of light is determined by the frequency, or rate of oscillation, of the light wave, which is determined by how energetically the charged particles that created the light vibrate. In the range of visible light, electromagnetic waves oscillate at frequencies from approximately 4.3×10^{14} hertz, or cycles per second, to 7.5×10^{14} hertz. That's a range of 430 trillion cycles per second for red light to 750 trillion cycles per second for blue light. Electromagnetic waves also have a wavelength, the distance from the crest of one wave to the crest of the next wave. The range of wavelengths for visible light is from 400 nanometers, or billionths of a meter (39.37 inches), for blue light to 700 nanometers for red light. Note how frequency and wavelength have an inverse proportional relationship; that is, as one quantity gets larger, the other quantity gets smaller. As wavelengths get shorter, frequency increases, and vice versa.

When a ray of sunlight passes through a prism, the different wavelengths proceed through at different velocities and the light is split into its component colors.

Dutch astronomer Christiaan Huygens believed that light was composed of waves.

The same process occurs when sunlight passes through water droplets in the sky. The sunlight is split into different wavelengths and the result is a rainbow. Newton had little understanding of this process when he first used a prism on a ray of sunlight. Newton in fact did not believe that light was made up of waves. A debate about the nature of light had been going on for some time. Newton's contemporary, Dutch astronomer Christiaan Huygens (1629–1695), believed that light was composed of waves. But Newton, observing that light traveled in straight lines and that it cast sharp shadows, decided that light must be composed of a stream of particles.

In 1802, English chemist William Wollaston (1766–1828) expanded on Newton's experiments with light and prisms. When Wollaston passed a beam of light through his prism, it yielded the expected bands of distinct colors, but he could see that there were several thin, dark lines scattered in the spectrum. Whether or not Newton saw these lines is uncertain, but Newton never mentioned them. Wollaston could not explain these dark lines and regarded them as natural boundaries between the different colors of light. The problem was taken up again in 1814 by Bavarian optician and instrument maker Joseph von Fraunhofer (1787–1826).

Fraunhofer's specialty was the manufacture of complex achromatic lenses that reduced chromatic aberration. With those skills, he was able to produce sharper

and easily read-
able spectrums.
When he exam-
ined a spectrum of
sunlight, he found
not just several
dark lines break-
ing up the colors,
but hundreds.
He counted 600 of
these lines and mapped
them. He began identifying
the most prominent lines with
letters of the alphabet. These are
now known as Fraunhofer lines. He noted that these
lines appeared in the exact same position in spectrums
from direct sunlight and sunlight reflected from the
Moon. He also placed a prism at the focal point of a
telescope and observed the spectrum of a star. He
noted that the dark lines were not in the same position
in the spectrum.

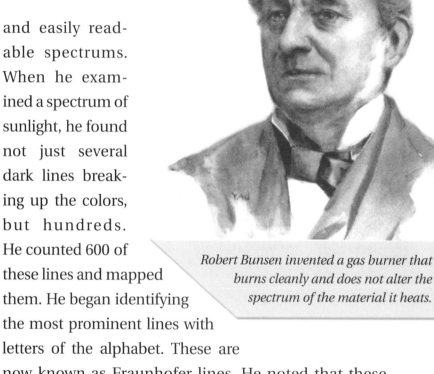

Robert Bunsen invented a gas burner that burns cleanly and does not alter the spectrum of the material it heats.

Gustav Kirchhoff helped design the first spectroscope.

THE SCIENCE OF SPECTROSCOPY

In 1860, two German scientists at the University of Heidelberg, Robert Bunsen (1811–1899) and Gustav Kirchhoff (1824–1887), devised the first spectroscope, a device containing a prism specifically designed to examine spectrums of light. They began to heat various materials to the point of incandescence, that is, until they began to glow and produce light. In this they were aided by Bunsen's earlier invention of a gas burner, now familiar to all high school science students, that burned cleanly. It produced a steady, faint light that did not interfere with or alter the spectrum of the material it was heating.

Bunsen burners are used extensively in scientific experiments and are a familiar sight in laboratories and high school science classrooms.

The first discovery that Kirchhoff and Bunsen made was that each chemical element produced its own unique set of lines. These lines were like fingerprints that identified the element that was being heated. Using pure metal samples, they recorded the spectral lines emitted by each element. Their work even led to the discovery of new metals, cesium and rubidium. What Kirchhoff and Bunsen were observing, however, were not dark lines, but bright lines of color. Further experiments revealed that there were two types of spectrums, emission and absorption spectrums. When an element was heated directly, in the Bunsen burner for example, it produced a distinctive set of colored lines. But when the incandescent light of some substance was projected through a colder gas, that gas absorbed the same frequencies of light that it would emit if directly heated, producing a spectrum full of dark lines instead of colored ones. This is known as Kirchhoff's law.

Kirchhoff noted that the element sodium produced a double colored line in the same position in its spectrum as a double dark line in the spectrum from the Sun. He concluded that light from the interior of the Sun was shining through the solar atmosphere, where sodium was absorbing light in the critical wavelengths that identified that element. Kirchhoff had discovered a method of identifying the

By studying the spectra of interstellar bodies, such as comets, scientists can determine the elements those bodies are composed of.

elements in stars. He identified about a half dozen other elements in the Sun's outer gaseous layers. Kirchhoff had disproved the famous statement of French philosopher Auguste Comte, who in 1835, when asked to give an example of the kind of knowledge humans would never obtain, referred to the composition of the stars.

A number of other scientists now began to look at the solar spectrum with its more than 600 lines, and by the end of the 1880s they had identified over fifty elements in the solar atmosphere. Swedish physicist Anders Angstrom (1814–1874) identified hydrogen in the Sun, and in 1868 created a map of the spectrum of visible light that precisely identified the location of more than a thousand spectral lines.

In England, astronomer William Huggins (1824–1910) studied the spectra of stars and nebulae and announced that they were mostly composed of hydrogen, and that everything in the universe was made from the same elements as could be found on Earth. Huggins also devised a method of attaching photographic equipment to his telescope and making permanent records of the spectra he observed. In Italy, astronomer Giovanni Donati (1826–1873) obtained the spectrum of a comet and proved that it contained carbon-based compounds.

COLOR AND TEMPERATURE

The work of Kirchhoff also attracted interest from Italian astronomer and Jesuit priest Angelo Secchi (1818–1878). Between 1863 and 1867, he observed the spectra from 4,000 stars and noted that differences in the dark lines in their spectra indicated that they varied in chemical composition. He decided to try to classify these stars according to the predominant colors in their spectra.

In Secchi's system, Type I stars are similar to the star Sirius and are bluish or whitish in color. Type II stars are solar, or sunlike, stars such as Arcturus and Capella, which radiate most of their light in the yellow part of the spectrum. Type III stars, similar to Betelgeuse, appear to be reddish in color. Type IV stars are also reddish in color but very dim. It was known that as the temperature of a very hot object increased, it changed color. Objects first glowed red, then orange, then yellow, and finally blue or white as

Star Type	Color	Approximate Surface Temperature	Average Mass (The Sun=1)	Average Luminosity (The Sun=1)	Examples
O	Blue	over 25,000 K	60	1,400,000	10 Lacertra
B	Blue	11,000-25,000 K	18	20,000	Rigel Spica
A	Blue	7,500-11,000 K	3.2	80	Sirius, Vega
F	Blue to White	6,000-7,5000 K	1.7	6	Canopus, Procyon
G	White to Yellow	5,000-6,000 K	1.1	1.2	Sun, Capella
K	Orange to Red	3,5000-5,000 K	0.8	0.4	Arcturus, Aldebaran
M	Red	under 3,500 K	0.3	0.04 (very faint)	Betelgeuse, Antares

This chart of spectral classes groups stars in series according to their temperatures. Our Sun is a G class star, with a surface temperature of about 5,000° to 6,000° Kelvin.

they became hotter. It seemed reasonable to suppose that the color of the stars was telling scientists something about their temperature.

Secchi's classification system was very crude and revealed very little about the nature of the stars, but it did stimulate scientists to study the differences between stars more carefully and to search for a system of classification that would explain the nature of these differences. In 1876, astronomer Edward Pickering (1846–1919) took over the observatory at Harvard University and began to study stellar spectra. Instead of focusing his telescope on one star at a time, he affixed a large prism to the instrument and took photographs of wide fields of stars. In this way he could record hundreds of spectra in one picture.

Pickering had the habit of hiring young women to do the grunt work of studying his photographs and classifying his spectra. In 1896, Radcliffe graduate Annie Jump Cannon (1863–1941) joined his team at Harvard. She discovered that spectra could be grouped into a continuous

Annie Jump Cannon discovered that spectra could be grouped into series that revealed the temperatures of stars.

series that revealed the temperature of their stars. She used the letters of the alphabet to classify the stars, in the sequence O, B, A, F, G, K, and M. The O stars were the hottest. Their surface temperatures were greater than 30,000° Kelvin. (A degree Kelvin is equal to a degree Celsius, but the Kelvin scale begins at -273.18° Celsius.) The interior temperature of the stars was presumed to be in the millions of degrees, of course, but only the surface temperatures could be measured. The M stars were relatively cool stars, with surface temperatures in the range of 2,000° to 3,500° Kelvin. Our own sun is a G class star, with a surface temperature of about 5,000° to 6,000° Kelvin. Between 1911 and 1914, Cannon classified the spectra of more than 220,000 stars, and these became the basis for Harvard's first catalog of stellar spectra, the Henry Draper Catalog. With some modifications, Cannon's classification system is still in use today.

The meaning of all this would be revealed by two scientists working independently in Europe and America, Danish astronomer Ejnar Hertzsprung (1873–1967) and American astronomer Henry Norris Russell (1877–1957). The relationship they would discover would become the foundation for the modern theory of how stars are born and how they die.

The Life Cycle of Stars

In 1909 Ejnar Hertzsprung arrived at the University of Gottingen in Denmark with a strong interest in the problem of stellar classification. He had tried to determine if there was a relationship between a star's color and its luminosity, that is, its brightness. There was a fundamental problem, however. You couldn't compare the brightness of two stars unless you knew how far away each one was. A very bright star might appear very dim because it was so much farther away than a closer, but not so bright, star. Measurements of stellar brightness date back to the Greek astronomer Hipparchus, who developed a scale of "magnitudes." He classified the twenty brightest stars in the sky as of the first magnitude, and stars of the sixth magnitude were the faintest stars still visible to the naked eye. In 1850, English astronomer Norman Pogson (1829–1891) noticed that on average, first magnitude stars were about 100 times as bright as sixth magnitude stars, and he worked out a formula whereby each whole number magnitude was approximately 2.5 times brighter than the next whole number magnitude. With this formula, astronomers could work out mathematically the brightness of many objects that were too faint to be seen without telescopes. Eventually magnitudes were determined more accurately with the aid of light-measuring instruments called photometers. Nevertheless, all these improvements only measured the brightness of stars without reference to their distance from the observer.

To solve this problem, Hertzsprung made a distinction between the "apparent magnitude" of a star's brightness and its "absolute magnitude." The apparent magnitude was simply how bright the star appeared to the naked eye from Earth. But absolute magnitude was how bright stars would appear if they were all viewed from a standard distance. The standard distance chosen by Hertzsprung was ten parsecs. A parsec represented a distance of 3.25 light years. To compare the brightness of stars, near stars would have to be moved farther away, to a distance of 32.5 light years, and distant stars would have to be moved closer. Of course, the stars could not really be moved, but if you knew how far away they were you could adjust their brightness by mathematical calculation. But how did astronomers know how far away the stars were?

Of course, astronomers did not know the distance to most of the stars, but they were able to creep up on the problem gradually by first determining the distance to some very near stars by using simple trigonometry and the phenomenon known as parallax. If you look at an object from two different locations, its position in your field of view will change. The simplest example of this is to hold your arm straight out in front of you and look at your raised thumb against a patterned background first with only your right eye and then with only your left eye. Think of your field of vision as a half circle of 180 degrees of arc. As you shift from one eye to the other, your thumb will appear to take up a new position against the background, shifting just a few degrees right and left. This angular shift in position is called parallax.

Parallax is often used to measure distances on the earth. A surveyor may look at a distant mountain from one position, and then move his apparatus a hundred yards away and take another measurement.

Trigonometry tells us that if you know the length of one side of a triangle, in this case called the base length, and you know the angles that the two other sides make with the base, you can calculate the length of the other two sides of the triangle. Of course, if an object is very far away, it will be very hard to measure the small shift in angular position. To do so, you need to view the object from two points that are much farther apart than your eyeballs. You need, in other words, a longer baseline. What is the longest baseline that astronomers can use? They could make two observations from observatories at opposite ends of a continent, creating a baseline of several thousand miles. Or they could make an observation of a star in January, and take another observation in June, when Earth had moved to the other side of its orbit, a baseline distance of 180 million miles! The distances to the nearest 100,000 stars can be determined by this method of triangulation.

Using ever increasing baselines, astronomers were able to determine the distances to some of the

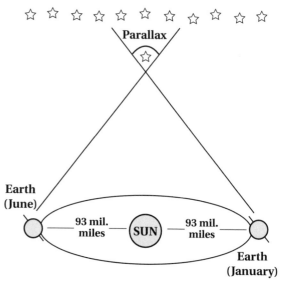

nearer stars. Once astronomers had accurate data for some stars, better techniques could be employed, using spectra to determine stellar type and comparing distant stars with the known absolute brightness of the nearer stars. By the time Hertzsprung and Russell tackled the problem, the distances to a fair number of near stars were known. Incidentally, it was this technique that defined the meaning of the parsec. A parsec is equal to one "parallax second." The angular shifts in the position of stars cannot be measured in whole degrees, because they are so far away. The angles must be measured in fractions

Parallax measures the apparent shift in position of a distant object when viewed from two separate locations.

of a degree. Each degree contains sixty subdivisions called minutes, and each minute contains sixty subdivisions called seconds. When the shift in angular position of a star is one parallax second, or one second of arc, the distance of that star to your baseline will be 3.25 light years, a distance defined as one parsec.

With a method of calculating the distances to the stars and formulas for adjusting that distance to a standard distance, Hertzsprung and Russell were ready to examine the relationship between a star's color and its luminosity. Each in his own country discovered the same relationship, that the color of a star and its absolute brightness were related. The hottest blue and white stars, the O class stars, were the brightest, though many of them appeared to be very small. The coolest red stars, the M stars, were the dimmest. The color of the stars responded to their temperature in the same way that a bar of metal changed color as it got hotter. Even more interesting, for most stars there seemed to be a direct correlation between their luminosity and their mass.

How did astronomers know the mass of the stars? How do you "weigh" a star? Fortunately, about half of the stars in the galaxy seem to be part of multiple star systems. It was German-English astronomer William Herschel (1738–1822) who in 1793 first demonstrated that there are stars that not only appear to be very close together in the sky, but are close together, and are actually gravitationally bound to each other. Herschel called them "binary stars." Binary stars are categorized by the method used to detect them. Visual binaries are double star systems in which the individual stars can be seen through a telescope, but a great many binaries are so close together and so distant from us that they cannot be separated by the finest telescopes. So other methods

William Herschel first discovered that many stars are paired and gravitationally bound to each other, and also figured out a way to measure the masses of many stars.

are used. Spectroscopic binaries are detected by the Doppler shifts in their spectrums. Eclipsing binaries are detected by variations in light that indicate a dimmer star is passing in front of a brighter star, or vice versa. The motions of many of these stars can be measured, their orbits figured out, and their mass calculated from the formulas for planetary motion worked out by Johannes Kepler (1571–1630) and the universal law of gravitation of Isaac Newton. The masses of many stars cannot be discovered in this way, but Hertzsprung and Russell had measurements for the mass of enough stars to make a useful statistical comparison of mass and luminosity.

The relationship that Hertzsprung and Russell discovered is generally plotted on a chart known as the Hertzsprung-Russell diagram. On the vertical axis of the diagram is plotted the luminosity or absolute brightness of a star, which is also a measure of its energy output. On the horizontal axis of the diagram is plotted the star's surface temperature, but unlike most such graphs or

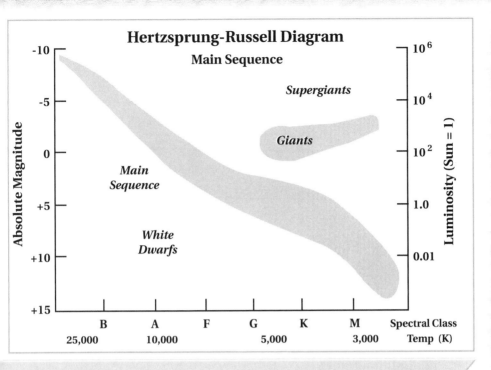

Hertzsprung-Russell Diagram

The higher a star appears on the Hertzsprung-Russell diagram, the brighter it is, and the farther to the left it appears, the hotter it is. Also, moving from right to left, the stars change color from red to yellow to blue to white.

charts, the highest temperatures are at the left side of the horizontal axis. The higher a star appears on this chart, the brighter it is, and the farther to the left it appears, the hotter it is. Also, moving from right to left, the stars change color from red to yellow to blue to white.

After they had plotted a sufficient number of stars on such a diagram, both Hertzsprung and Russell were struck by an obvious pattern that emerged. Yes, there were some bright but cool, reddish stars, now known as red giants, in the upper right of the diagram, and there were some very small but extremely bright stars, now known as white dwarfs, in the lower left corner of the diagram. But the majority of the stars, more than 90 percent, of whatever color or temperature, fell along a diagonal line that ran from the upper left to the lower right of the diagram. And the mass of the stars was seen to increase as you moved up and to the left on this diagonal line. This diagonal line was named the "main sequence," and stars on the main sequence got hotter and brighter as they became more massive. At the right end of the main sequence could be found relatively small reddish and yellow stars with cooler surface temperatures. The Sun was such a star, known as a yellow dwarf. At the left end of the main sequence could be found more massive stars with higher surface temperatures that burned blue or white. Along the main sequence, the more massive a star was, the hotter and brighter it burned. For most of the stars, the property of mass seemed to be the variable that controlled how the stars shone.

The neatness of this relationship between mass and brightness and color tempted Russell to develop a theory of how stars evolve. Russell's theory was not correct, but it was a significant step in the right direction. Russell thought that a star first evolved from a cloud of hydrogen gas collapsing under its own gravitational attraction. So far so good. But he thought that the red giants represented this first stage of collapse, with the gas beginning to glow red under increasing pressure and heat. Russell thought that as the material of the star continued to contract, it got hotter and brighter until it became a smaller, yellow star, and then moved up the line of the main sequence, becoming a hotter, brighter, blue-white star. When the star exhausts its hydrogen fuel and begins to cool, it moves back down the line of the main sequence, becoming a yellow star again, then a red dwarf, and then a burnt out cinder.

Both Hertzsprung and Russell had discovered a fundamental relationship between a star's mass and how it burned. But the discoveries came before the great breakthroughs in the understanding of the atom and the nature of nuclear energy in

Arthur Eddington discovered that the balance between gravity and radiation keeps stars from collapsing.

the early twentieth century, and so they were not able to correctly interpret the meaning of their data.

The problem was taken up by English astronomer and physicist Arthur Stanley Eddington (1882–1944). Eddington knew that a star was simply a ball of mostly hydrogen gas, and he was trying to understand what prevented this ball of gas from

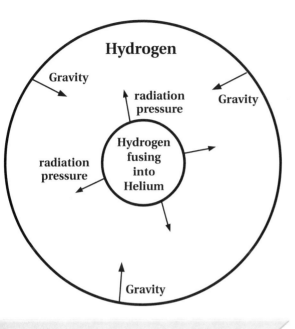

This is an interior cross section of a main sequence star. If gravity and radiation pressure are equal, it is stable.

collapsing into a very small and compact mass. Why, Eddington asked, weren't all stars white dwarfs? His answer was that while the material of stars was collapsing under the influence of gravity, whatever process at the heart of a star made it burn, this process generated tremendous amounts of radiation and heat that created an outward pressure that balanced the gravitational collapse. The more massive a star, the greater the internal pressure caused by gravity, and therefore the greater the outward radiation pressure. Consequently, the more massive a star was, the more luminous it would appear. As long as a

star had adequate fuel to burn, it would maintain this balance between gravity and radiation pressure and shine at a steady rate. This is what the stars on the main sequence were doing. The bigger stars at the left end of the main sequence burned more brightly but were using up their fuel at a faster rate. The smaller stars at the right end of the main sequence were not as bright but burned fuel at a slower rate and had longer lives than bigger stars. All the stars on the main sequence, however, were in the prime of their lives, burning evenly and steadily.

Eddington announced his confirmation of the mass-luminosity relationship in 1924, and by this time a revolution in scientific thinking had taken place. At the turn of the century, French physicists Antoine-Henri Becquerel (1852–1908) and Marie Curie (1867–1934)

Marie Curie helped discover radioactivity, which ultimately led to our understanding of how stars generate energy.

had discovered radioactivity. By 1914, Ernest Rutherford (1871–1937) had discovered that the indivisible atom was in fact made up of sub- atomic particles, and it was probable that some force greater than electromagnetism held

Hans Bethe discovered that nuclear fusion is what makes stars shine.

these particles together. In 1905 Albert Einstein (1879–1955) had published his special theory of relativity, and in 1916 he published his general theory of relativity. It was now known that mass and energy were equivalent, and that a small amount of mass can be converted into an enormous amount of energy. By the 1940s scientists in the United States had designed and tested an atomic bomb that was proof of the power of the nuclear forces binding subatomic particles.

German-American physicist Hans Bethe (1906–) had worked on the atomic bomb project, but the energy released by these bombs was the result of a process known as nuclear fission, the splitting apart of atomic nucleii by bombardment by energetic neutrons. That process did not seem to be operating in the stars, but in 1938 Bethe proposed another method by which a star might release huge amounts of energy. In a process known as nuclear fusion, atoms of hydrogen at the center of a star, under huge temperatures and pressures, will fuse together into helium atoms, converting about 1 percent of their mass into energy. For a star like the Sun to produce the energy it does through fusion, it would have to convert more than four million tons of hydrogen into pure energy every second. But that is not a problem for a body with as much hydrogen as a star has. Bethe had worked out the mechanism by which a cloud of hydrogen gas under gravitational compression

could generate prodigious amounts of energy for millions or billions of years. Bethe had finally answered the question of how the stars shine.

Fusion is a difficult process to initiate. To force the nucleii of two hydrogen atoms close enough together to fuse them, you must overcome the electromagnetic force that causes the two positively charged protons to repel each other. Ordinarily, the electromagnetic force is much stronger than the force of gravity. The reason that you do not sink into the middle of the earth, in spite of the earth's gravity, is that the negatively charged electrons in the atoms of your shoe are repelled by the negatively charged electrons in the atoms of the ground. This force is sufficient to overcome the earth's force of gravity. It takes a massive body like a star to provide a force of gravitational attraction strong enough to overcome electromagnetism and push protons together.

It remained for other scientists to work out the correct sequence of a star's evolution. It is now believed that most stars begin their life cycle on the main sequence as contracting clouds of hydrogen gas. When gravity has compressed the interior of this gas cloud to a certain point, nuclear fusion begins and the star begins to shine. An equilibrium is established between the gravitational force of the star and the outward radiation pressure. The star ceases to contract and burns in a steady fashion for as long as it has fuel. When, after millions or billions of years, a star runs out of hydrogen fuel, its interior layers collapse while its outer layers explode outward. This is known as a nova. This produces a very large but diffuse cloud of gas still giving off heat, but at a much lower temperature, and radiating light in the red part of the spectrum. This explains the existence of red giants. They are not the birth stage of stars, as Russell believed, but a stage in the death of stars. During this violent process of burning out, the plot of a star will take it up and out of the main sequence into the upper right corner of the Hertzsprung-Russell diagram, where the red giants are

found. Stars like Betelgeuse, Antares, and Arcturus are examples of red giants.

As the red giant begins to cool, gravity becomes more powerful than outward radiation pressure, and the star begins to collapse again. The outer layers of the red giant are blown away into space, and the smaller stellar mass contracts into a tiny, hotter white dwarf star. When plotted on the Hertzsprung-Russell diagram, the red giant migrates to the lower left, where white dwarfs are located. White dwarfs are no longer producing energy through the process of fusion. They are like brightly glowing embers, but they will eventually burn out completely and cease to give off any light. A white dwarf is a very dense star, but it is only a few times the diameter of Earth in size. This

A supernova occurs at the end of a star's life, when its nuclear fuel is spent. Its core collapses and releases a huge amount of energy, causing a blast wave that ejects the star's gaseous envelope into interstellar space.

whole process was first described by astronomer Fred Hoyle (1915–). He demonstrated that the Hertzsprung-Russell diagram, correctly interpreted, was a guide to the evolution of stars from birth to death. These very different types of stars, main sequence stars, red giants, white dwarfs, were different stages in the life cycle of those stars.

Very massive stars, when they have used up their hydrogen fuel, undergo particularly violent explosions known as supernovae. These explosions generate an enormous amount of energy and often push a huge cloud of gas outward from the star. From Earth, this cloud is seen as a ring around the star, and it is called a planetary nebula. The gas cloud travels outward from the star and will, given enough time, "seed" interstellar space with the heavy elements created in the explosion.

Astronomers and physicists had finally taken all the painstakingly acquired data about different types of stars and made order out of that data. They

Most stars are born in contracting clouds of hydrogen gas. When gravity has compressed the interior of these gas clouds to a certain point, nuclear fusion occurs and the star begins to shine.

understood the physical process within stars that produced so much energy, and they understood why stars had different temperatures and came in different colors. They understood a lot. But there were still surprises to come.

4

Stars That Don't Shine

Astronomers had learned that the most fundamental property of stars was their mass. The mass, the amount of material in the original cloud of hydrogen gas that collapsed to form the star, determined how hot it would burn, what color it would be, where on the main sequence it would

appear, and how long the star would continue to shine. Medium to smallish size stars, like our own sun, known to astronomers as dwarf stars, would shine for 10 to 15 to 20 billion years, then flare up in a

A portion of the ring of gas that forms around a star that has supernovaed.

nova to produce a cooler red giant, and then burn out as white dwarfs. But what was the fate of the more massive stars? Most of the stars in our galaxy are dwarf stars, but there are plenty of stars that are much bigger. Deneb in the constellation Cygnus (the Swan) is classified as a blue supergiant star that is a million times more luminous than our sun. Rigel in the constellation Orion is another blue supergiant, more than 100 times bigger than our sun. We know that because of the greater gravitational pressures at their cores, more massive stars burn their hydrogen fuel more quickly than smaller stars, and therefore have shorter lives. Whereas our sun, halfway through its life cycle on the main sequence, will shine steadily for another five billion years, a massive star like Rigel will exhaust its hydrogen fuel in no more than another two million years. What happens to such stars?

Astronomer Fred Hoyle theorized that with massive stars, even after their hydrogen fuel was exhausted and they entered the red giant phase, there was enough gravitational pressure to keep the fusion process going. But with the star's supply of hydrogen depleted and converted into helium, it was now the helium that fused into nuclei of carbon and oxygen atoms. If the star was massive enough, these elements continued fusing into heavier elements like magnesium, sulfur, and finally iron. In this way, layers of the heavy elements were created in the cores of massive stars. But what happened then?

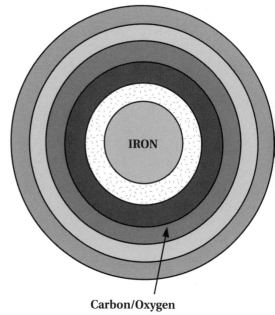

IRON

Carbon/Oxygen

A massive star has many layers in which different elements are created by fusion.

RADIO ASTRONOMY

The answer did not come until astronomers had developed a new tool to study the unseen energy of the stars. Stars radiate energy not only in the range of visible light, but all across the electromagnetic spectrum. Before 1930, astronomy was mainly concerned with visible light. But in 1932, radio engineer Karl Jansky (1905–1950) was asked by his employer, Bell Telephone Laboratories, to investigate the problem of static in radio communications. There were many causes of radio static, such as electrical storms and interference from other electric devices. But when Jansky had accounted for all these

Karl Jansky detected the first extraterrestrial source of radio emission coming from the area of the Sagittarius constellation.

types of interference, he found that his antenna was still picking up a faint unexplained form of static. Its source moved across the sky at the same rate as the apparent motion of the stars, and seemed to be located somewhere in the constellation Sagittarius. Other astronomers had identified this region as the probable location of the center of the galaxy. Jansky had detected the first extraterrestrial source of radio emission.

Jansky's work attracted the attention of another American radio engineer, Grote Reber (1911–). In 1937, Reber built the first real radio telescope in his backyard, a parabolic "dish" antenna thirty-one feet in diameter that could be pointed in different directions. Reber spent the next ten years making a map of the intensity of radio signals in the sky. He discovered numerous "radio stars"—stars that emitted radio waves but could not be found through optical telescopes. In 1951, English astronomer Bernard Lovell (1913–) began construction of the first large radio telescope at Jodrell Bank, England. It was 250 feet in

Scientists realized that radio telescopes could be used to track artificial satellites such as Sputnik, above.

diameter and used the turret mechanism from a battleship to move the dish. Lovell was widely criticized for spending so much money on such an esoteric device, but the Jodrell Bank radio telescope was finished in time for the Russian launching of Sputnik, and his critics realized how valuable such an instrument would be in tracking artificial satellites. Radio

Radio telescopes sweep the cosmos looking for new interstellar phenomena, as well as signs of life.

astronomy is today one of the most productive methods of studying the cosmos, and hundreds of large radio telescopes have been constructed all around the world. The radio telescope has the advantage of working day or night, regardless of whether the stars are visible, and whether or not there are clouds in the sky.

Radio pulses from a Pulsar

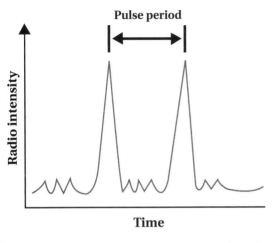

Pulse period

Radio intensity

Time

Pulsars emit short bursts of radio energy at regular intervals.

PULSARS

In 1967, a Cambridge University graduate student, Jocelyn Bell (1943–), working with a radio telescope she and other university students built, detected a peculiar radio signal coming from somewhere between the stars Vega and Altair. She called in her thesis adviser, astronomer Anthony Hewish (1924–), and they began to study the signal. What made it so peculiar was its regularity. It consisted of a series of pulses, or short bursts of radio energy, that were exactly one and a third seconds apart, like the regular ticking of a clock. Other such pulsing objects were

The pulses of a pulsar are caused by rotating beams of energy.

soon discovered in different regions of the sky. The interval between pulses may vary, but it was always measured in seconds or fractions of seconds, and the pulsation was always regular. Such a rapid, regular signal was unheard of in astronomy, and for a time, though not very seriously, the investigators referred to their discovery as an LGM, which stood for "little green men," as if they were receiving a beacon of some kind from an extraterrestrial civilization. If such a signal had not clearly revealed itself as coming from the sky, Bell and Hewish would have instantly assumed it was man-made interference.

The Pulsar Lighthouse Effect

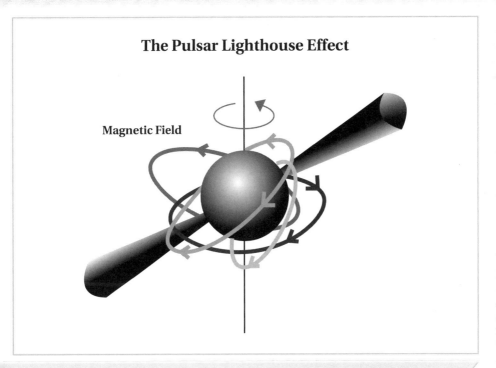

Magnetic Field

As a massive star collapses, it rotates faster, emitting huge streams of radiation. These are funneled into narrow beams by the star's magnetic field, and spin along with the star, like beams of light from a lighthouse.

Hewish quickly ruled out the possibility of extraterrestrial intelligence by studying the radio signal for a Doppler shift. In 1842, Austrian physicist Christian Doppler (1803–1853) had discovered that waves—sound or light—emanating from an object moving toward or away from the observer would shift in frequency. If the object was moving away from you,

the waves would stretch out and arrive at a lower frequency. If the object was moving toward you, its waves would pile up against each other and arrive at a higher frequency. Hewish reasoned that if the signal was the work of intelligent beings living on a planet orbiting a distant star, small changes in the frequency of the radio waves ought to reveal the movement of the planet in its orbit. No such movement was detected. And yet a signal that pulsed so quickly could not be a signal from the surface of a star. Stars were rather large bodies. It took time for bursts of radiation like this to build up in stars, and no stars were known that could rotate so rapidly that they could produce such a rapidly pulsating signal. All the same, when he published his findings, Hewish called the radio source a pulsating star, or a "pulsar."

The explanation was provided by astronomer Thomas Gold of Cornell University in the early 1970s. Gold said that a pulsar was a "neutron star," and suddenly there was new insight into what happened to very massive stars. For very massive stars, the white dwarf stage was not the last stage of their existence. There was just too much mass involved, and after the red giant stage, which for these kinds of stars involved a powerful "supernova" explosion, massive stars just went on collapsing under tremendous gravitational force. As early as 1939, Indian American astronomer Subrahmanyan Chandrasekhar (1910–1995) had calculated that stars more than 1.5 times as massive as the Sun could not end their lives as white dwarfs. A white dwarf, as dense as it is, ceases to collapse because the negatively charged electrons in its atoms repel each other, and this force is stronger than the star's gravity. But if a star is between four to eight times as massive as the Sun, the gravitational force is strong enough to overcome the resistance of the electrons and literally push them inside the protons of the atomic nuclei. This is a state known as "electron degeneracy." When a proton and an electron are forced together, their opposite electric charges cancel

out and they produce a particle with no electric charge and the mass of a neutron. In this super dense state, the entire star consists of nothing but neutrons. At least that was Chandrasekhar's theory in 1939. Now Bell and Hewish had actually detected such a star. But how were these pulses produced?

With gravity stronger than the repulsive force of its electrons, a massive star of this type went on collapsing until it was no more than about ten kilometers (six miles) in diameter. From a size many times larger than the Sun, such a star collapses into an object smaller than a medium-sized asteroid. Since angular momentum is conserved, as the star gets smaller it must rotate faster and faster, like a ballet dancer or ice skater who pulls in her arms and spins more rapidly. The tremendous forces involved cause the star to emit huge streams of radiation, including radio waves, which are funneled into narrow beams by the star's magnetic field, and which spin along with the star like the beams from a lighthouse. If there is just the right

This dramatic image from the Hubble telescope reveals a pair of fiery lobes protruding from a dying star that was once the size of our Sun.

alignment between the neutron star's spin and an observer on Earth, a radio telescope will detect the beam as a pulse of radio energy with each rapid rotation of the star. The discovery of a new type of star made up of superdense matter helped to complete the theoretical picture of stellar evolution. But there were even stranger objects in the heavens yet to be

discovered and explained. What if one asked, for example, what happened to dying stars that were more than eight times as massive as the Sun?

THE LIGHT THAT FAILED

Albert Einstein's general theory of relativity, introduced in 1916, was in essence a new theory of gravity. It replaced Isaac Newton's theory that gravity was a force of attraction acting on all bodies with the idea that bodies caused distortions or curvatures in space-time. All objects, including waves of light, when moving through these curvatures of space-time, had to move in curved paths, and gave the appearance of being under the influence of a force. With this new conception of space-time as something that could bend, it was not difficult for scientists to imagine objects with such concentrated mass that space-time could be completely folded in on itself around such massive objects. German astronomer Karl

Schwarzchild (1873–1916) was serving on the Russian front as an artilleryman in World War I when he heard of Einstein's work. In the last year of his life, Schwarzchild began to calculate what would happen to a very massive object that collapsed. Remember that a neutron star is formed when gravity overcomes the electromagnetic force. But the collapse stops at a certain point, and the neutron star still has physical dimensions, because of complex physical forces that keep the neutrons apart. But if the mass of the collaps- ing star is great enough, gravity will overcome even these forces, and all the matter in the star, as Schwarzchild noted, would collapse and keep on col- lapsing until it reached an infinitesimally small point. This was called a "singularity." Theoretically, this mass now occupies no volume at all, and, according to general relativity, time stops completely at this point.

Light, or any electromagnetic radiation emitted by such a body, would encounter a region of space- time completely folded around the collapsed object,

and would endlessly circle that object, unable to escape into space. There would be a region of space around the singularity from which no object, including light, could escape if it ventured too close, and that boundary of no return was called an "event horizon." The radius of the event horizon depended on how much mass was in the collapsed object, though regardless of the amount of mass, the object was always a single point in space. Because no light could escape from such objects, American physicist John Wheeler (1911–) named them "black holes." In theory, here was an explanation, admittedly a very bizarre explanation, for what might happen to stars eight or more times more massive than the Sun when they finally exploded in a supernova and collapsed.

If the mass of a collapsing star is large enough, all the matter in the star collapses until it reaches a "singularity." Its gravitational attraction is so strong that, after passing the event horizon, even light cannot escape.

Black holes were stars that did not shine. But did black holes exist?

How do you find something that you can't see? Black holes may not emit light, but they still have powerful gravitational fields, and remember that at least half of the stars in the heavens are part of binary or multiple star systems. If a black hole and another star were orbiting each other closely, the gravity of the black hole would pull in gas and dust from the other star. Under the influence of this intense gravitational field, the gas and dust would spiral in toward the event horizon. Compression and frictional forces will heat this gas and dust to the point where it will give off intense radiation in the range of X rays, and these X rays can be detected. You cannot see the black hole itself, but if it is orbiting another star, you can see the radiation from the ring of matter being sucked in toward the event horizon. X rays, incidentally, cannot penetrate Earth's atmosphere, so the search for black holes could not take place until we were able to put detecting satellites into orbit.

STARS THAT DON'T SHINE

In the early 1970s, a source of X ray emissions was discovered in the constellation Cygnus near the star known as HDE 226868. HDE 226868 was a blue supergiant star, and Doppler shifts in its spectrum indicated that it was orbiting another object every 5.6 days. Careful observations revealed that the companion object was the likely source of the X rays. It was designated Cygnus X-1, as the first such X-ray source discovered in this constellation. Though the companion object itself was not visible, and orbital analysis indicated that it was very small in size, its gravitational effect on HDE 226868 was such that it had to be about eight times the mass of the Sun. Astronomers moved cautiously because they were dealing with such a strange object, but they are now about 95 percent certain that Cygnus X-1 is a black hole, the first one to be detected. Many other potential black holes have since been found, and in fact astronomers now believe that most galaxies have huge black holes at their centers.

SUPERNOVAE

We owe our very existence to the explosion and collapse of such massive stars. The very young universe was composed mostly of hydrogen and a little helium. We have seen how some of the simpler elements like carbon, oxygen, and iron can be created in the interior of stars during the fusion process. But when massive stars explode, the pressures and temperatures created by the explosion fuse subatomic particles into even heavier elements, all the way up to uranium. This is how all the heavier elements are created and how they diffuse through the universe as explosive debris to eventually form planets and human beings. The creation and diffusion of heavier elements across the universe takes

Population I stars are found in the arms of a spiral galaxy. Population II stars are found in the halos and globular clusters that surround a spiral galaxy.

time, of course, as well as many supernova explosions, but the universe is 15 billion years old, more than enough time for this process to take place.

Evidence for this process was discovered in the 1940s by German American astronomer Walter Baade (1893–1960). Baade immigrated to the United States in 1931. During World War II, the city of Los Angeles was blacked out at night. Thus, viewing conditions for astronomers were the best they had been in decades. Working at the Mount Wilson observatory near the city, Baade was able to carefully study individual stars in the Andromeda galaxy, a spiral galaxy relatively close to our Milky Way galaxy and similar in size and shape. Baade discovered two distinct types of stars, which he classified as Population I and Population II stars. Population I stars were found mostly in the spiral arms of Andromeda's disk. They were young stars, formed between 1 and 100 million years ago. The spectra from these stars revealed that they were rich in heavier elements. Population II stars were found mostly in the halos and globular clusters that surrounded Andromeda. They were older stars, formed from 1 to 15 billion years ago, and did not contain significant amounts of heavy elements. It was clear that the earlier generations of stars were lacking metals and heavy elements because they had not yet been created by successive supernova explosions. Younger stars, however, formed in an environment rich in heavy elements created by the explosive deaths of the earlier stars. Two points became clear at once. Only young star systems had the materials to create rocky, terrestrial-type planets, and stars with terrestrial-type planets would probably only form in the spiral arms of galaxies, where the younger stars were forming.

Our Sun

5

So what do we know about our own sun, the only star close enough to us to appear as something more than a bright point in the sky? The Sun is an average star. It is a G class star, or a yellow dwarf. It condensed from hydrogen gas and dust (particles of heavier elements) and ignited about 5 billion years ago. We know that the Sun is a Population I star, because the primordial gas cloud that formed it contained enough dust to also form the rocky planets. The Sun is composed of about 94 percent hydrogen and about 5.9 percent helium, with a trace amount of other elements. The Sun still contains enough hydrogen to continue its fusion reactions for about another five billion years. As the Sun uses up its hydrogen it will expand into a red giant. When that happens, the diameter of the Sun will expand to engulf the planet Venus, and possibly even Earth.

The Sun can be thought of as consisting of six layers. Starting at the center and moving outward, these layers are the core, the radiative zone, the convective zone, the photosphere, the chromosphere, and the corona. The core of the Sun is where nuclear fusion takes place. The core has a diameter of about 400,000 kilometers (249,000 miles), or about 10 percent of the Sun's radius. The temperature of the core is about 15,000,000°C (28,000,000°F). Each second, about 700,000,000 tons of hydrogen are converted into about 650,000,000 tons of helium. The difference is the amount of mass converted into energy.

Outside the core is the radiative zone, a layer of hydrogen and helium gas that conducts heat from the core to the convective zone. The radiative zone is about 300,000 kilometers (186,000 miles) thick. The energy released from fusion reactions takes thousands of years to make its way out of this layer. Photons of electromagnetic energy jump from atom to atom in the dense stellar material, eventually reaching the Sun's outer layers. The first layer above the radiative zone is the convective zone, where heat is transferred by convection, or the fluid movement of the Sun's matter. The convective zone is about 200,000 kilometers (124,000 miles) thick.

Above the convective zone is the photosphere. The photosphere is considered the lowest layer of the solar atmosphere. It is the layer from which most of the Sun's visible light is emitted. It is what we see when we look at the Sun. The temperature of the photosphere is about 5,500°C (10,000°F), making it much cooler than the inner layers. The photosphere is about 600 kilometers (370 miles) thick. When astronomers observe the photosphere, they see a granulated surface resembling the surface of boiling water. These are the tops of the columns of rising gas coming up from the convective zone. Each granule is about 1,000 kilometers across. Sometimes cooler and darker blotches appear on the surface of the photosphere. These are magnetic storms called sunspots. Sunspot activity increases and decreases in an eleven-year cycle. Scientists still do not know why this occurs.

Above the photosphere is the chromosphere, a jagged layer about 10,000 kilometers thick with a temperature of about 15,000°C, hotter than the underlying photosphere. When observed edge-on during a solar eclipse, the chromosphere appears

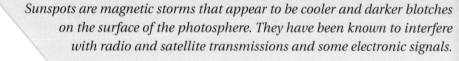

Sunspots are magnetic storms that appear to be cooler and darker blotches on the surface of the photosphere. They have been known to interfere with radio and satellite transmissions and some electronic signals.

pinkish and consists of numerous flame-like spikes called spicules. In addition to these spicules, sometimes huge flares and loops of hot gas shoot up from the chromosphere, extending into the outer layer of the Sun's atmosphere, the corona. The gases that make up the corona are only visible during a total solar eclipse. The corona extends outward from the

Sun for a distance equal to ten to twelve times its diameter. The temperature in the Sun's corona is about two million degrees Kelvin, but because there are so few atoms in the corona, not much heat energy is contained here. The corona is less than one-billionth the density of Earth's atmosphere and is, for all practical purposes, almost a vacuum. But when viewed during an eclipse it is filled with visible plumes and streamers of gas that are quite dramatic.

Recent studies have revealed that the corona really doesn't end abruptly, but thins out as it extends far out into the solar system, reaching as far as Saturn and perhaps farther. In this form it is known as the "solar wind," and consists of streams of charged particles (ions and electrons) racing outward from the Sun at increasing speeds. The particles take about ten days to reach Earth, at which time they are traveling at about 400 kilometers per second. The particles are captured by Earth's magnetic field and are pulled toward the North and South Poles, where they are accelerated and release visible radiation, creating auroras.

THE SUN'S ENERGY

We measure the Sun's energy output in terms that are meaningful to us here on Earth, and we call this measurement the "solar constant." This is a measure of the amount of energy that passes through a square centimeter at Earth's average distance from the Sun. This has been determined to be about two calories per cubic centimeter every minute. Don't confuse these calories with the calories you measure in your food. Those are really kilocalories, 1,000 times greater than

This chart compares absolute (real) brightness with apparent brightness, which depends on a star's distance from Earth.

Rank	Star	Absolute Magnitude	Apparent Magnitude	Distance from Earth (light-years)
.	The Sun	+4.8	-26.72	.
1	Sirius	+1.4	-1.46	8.6
2	Canopus	-2.5	-0.72	74
3	Rigel Kantaurus	+4.4	-0.27	4.3
4	Arcturus	+0.2	-0.04	34
5	Vega	+0.6	0.03	25
6	Capella	+0.4	+0.08	41
7	Rigel	-8.1	+0.12	1,400
8	Procyon	2.8	+0.38	11
9	Archenar	-1.3	+0.46	75
10	Betelgeuse	-7.2	+0.50	1,500
11	Hadar	-4.3	+0.61	300
12	Altair	+2.3	+0.77	17
13	Acrux	-3.8	+0.79	270
14	Aldebaran	-0.2	+0.85	65
15	Antares	-4.5	+0.96	400
20	Deneb	-7.2	+1.25	1,500
—	Proxima Centauri	+15.5	+11.05 (var.)	4.3

the calorie used by physicists. Two calories per square centimeter per minute is equivalent to about 0.135 watts per cubic centimeter. A satellite orbiting Earth with a solar panel of 1,000 square centimeters (about 160 square inches) would, if it could convert such energy with 100 percent efficiency, have a power source of a little more than one watt. Measurements of solar energy output are important to our understanding of Earth's weather and climate. It is also important to understand that the Sun is the source of all of our energy. Weather processes driven by heat from the Sun create the energy in the movement of wind and water, and the energy in coal and oil is stored solar energy.

About five billion years from now, when the Sun runs out of its supply of hydrogen fuel and the fusion reactions in its core cease, it will explode into a huge thin cloud of gas that radiates most of its light in the red region of the spectrum. This gas will be much cooler than present temperatures on the surface of the Sun, but still hot enough to scorch Earth, burn away its atmosphere, and destroy all life on Earth. Will some human beings be able to travel to planets on other stars and escape Earth's fate? Will there even be a human civilization on earth that far in the future? These questions cannot be answered. What is certain is that from its bloated red giant stage, the Sun will shrink into a white dwarf, a bright, dying ember of a star. And then it will wink out. It will become a cold, dark ball of hydrogen and helium gas without the gravitational density to restart the fusion process and blaze into light. On Earth and all the other planets, there will no longer be day and night. The skies will be perpetually dark, and Earth will be cold and desolate. As all things come to an end, so too will the light from the stars.

Glossary

absolute magnitude The brightness of a star as measured from a standard distance.

apparent magnitude The brightness of a star measured without consideration of its distance from the observer.

black hole Produced from the explosion and collapse of a massive star, an object that exerts a gravitational force so strong that even light cannot escape from it.

Doppler effect The apparent change in the frequency of waves from an object that is moving toward or away from an observer.

electromagnetic spectrum All the wavelengths of electromagnetic radiation from radio waves to gamma rays.

Hertzsprung-Russell diagram A graph showing the relationship between a star's luminosity and its surface temperature, color, and mass.

light year A unit equal to the distance that light travels in one year.

luminosity The amount of light energy emitted by a star. Its absolute magnitude.

main sequence The diagonal plot of stars on the Hertsprung-Russell diagram that reveals the relationship of their mass, color, temperature, and luminosity.

neutron star The compacted remains of a massive star that has undergone a supernova and collapse, in which its electrons and protons have fused into neutrons. If the

energy from a rotating neutron star can be detected on Earth, it is called a pulsar.

nuclear fusion The process by which atomic nuclei fuse together to form a larger nucleus, releasing a great amount of energy. This is how stars generate light and heat.

parallax The apparent angular shift in the position of a distant object when viewed from different positions.

prism A triangular piece of glass that splits light into its different wavelengths.

pulsar A rapidly spinning neutron star that emits pulses of electromagnetic radiation.

red giant A star that has expanded and cooled after using up its hydrogen fuel.

spectroscopy The study of spectral lines and color distribution in the light from incandescent objects.

spectrum The rainbow of colors produced when white light is passed through a prism.

supernova The powerful explosion that occurs when a massive star uses up its hydrogen fuel.

white dwarf A small, hot star near the end of its life.

For More Information

SCIENTIFIC ORGANIZATIONS

American Astronomical Society
2000 Florida Avenue NW, Suite 400
Washington, DC 20009-1231
(202) 328-2010
Web site: http://www.aas.org

The Astronomical Society of the Pacific
390 Ashton Avenue
San Francisco, CA 94112
(415) 337-1100
Web site: http://www.aspsky.org

National Aeronautics and Space Administration (NASA)

Web site: http://www.nasa.gov

WEB SITES

StarDate Online

http://stardate.utexas.edu

This is the Web site for the University of Texas' McDonald Observatory's StarDate radio series and magazine. This Web site has a searchable index of all the radio transcripts as well as star-watching information and star charts.

Earth and Sky

http://www.earthsky.com

This is the Web site for the Earth and Sky radio series. The Web site has a searchable index of transcripts for its shows and additional background information for each show.

Hawaiian Astronomical Society

http://www.hawastsoc.org

This Web site has almost everything anyone wants to know about the sun. The site has cross sections, photographs, animations, and more.

Space Telescope Science Institute

http://www.stsci.edu

This is the homepage for the Hubble Space Telescope. The Web site has an archive of photos, description of scientific instruments, and a wealth of other information.

For Further Reading

Berman, Bob. *Secrets of the Night Sky: The Most Amazing Things in the Universe You Can See with the Naked Eye.* New York: Harper Perennial, 1996.

Chartrand, Mark R. *National Audubon Society Field Guide to the Night Sky.* New York: Alfred A. Knopf, 1991.

Consolmagno, Guy, and Dan M. Davis. *Turn Left at Orion: A Hundred Night Sky Objects to See in a Small Telescope—and How to Find Them,* 3rd ed. New York: Cambridge University Press, 2000.

Dickinson, Terence. *Nightwatch: A Practical Guide to Viewing the Universe,* 3rd ed. Buffalo, NY: Firefly Books, 1998.

Engelbert, Phillis, and Diane L. Dupuis. *The Handy Space Answer Book.* Detroit: Visible Ink Press, 1998.

Moore, Patrick. *Stargazing: Astronomy Without a Telescope,* 2nd ed. New York: Cambridge University Press, 2001.

Raymo, Chet. *365 Starry Nights: An Introduction to Astronomy for Every Night of the Year.* New York: Simon and Schuster, 1992.

Index

Credits

ABOUT THE AUTHOR

Allan B. Cobb is a freelance science editor who lives in central Texas. He has written books, articles, radio scripts, and educational materials concerning different aspects of science. When not writing about science, he enjoys traveling, camping, hiking, and exploring caves.

PHOTO CREDITS

Cover © A. Caulet (ST-ECF, ESA), and NASA; cover inset © E. J. West/Index Stock; cover inset and p. 70 © E.J. West/Index Stock Imagery; pp. 8, 18, 24, 26, 27 © North Wind Picture Archives; pp. 10, 44, 53, 69 © Archive Photos; pp. 11, 12 © Bettmann/Corbis; p. 14 © Jim Sugar Photography/Corbis; pp. 16–17 © Enzo & Paolo Ragazzin/Corbis; p. 28 © Cris Salvo/FPG; p. 30 © Jerry

DESIGN AND LAYOUT

Evelyn Horovicz